Yes-but®

Flip-thin

Berthold Gunster

Original title **Omder**

Translation **Chris King Perryman**
Graphic Design **Jan Gunster**

ISBN 978 94 005 0583 4
NUR 770

Fourth impression, July 2019

When it's windy some people build windscreens.

Others build windmills.

Stuck-thinking

When we are confronted with a problem – whatever that problem may be, a rebellious child, a rainy vacation, a malfunctioning body part - our first reaction is 'yes-but'. We want to get rid of it.

A yes-but reaction is logical and understandable, nobody welcomes a problem. But the effect of a yes-but reaction can be disappointing and in most cases the situation goes from bad to worse. When we resist a problem it tends to turn into a disaster, what the Germans call a 'Verschlimbesserung'.

However as neither the English nor the Dutch language provides a word which adequately expresses this idea, we made one up, 'vastdenken' or 'stuck-thinking'.

Stuck-thinking examples come in all shapes and sizes. Social geographers know it as the waterbed effect. For example when you improve living conditions in a certain neighbourhood without improving the adjacent areas, the problems will probably shift to those surrounding areas, rather like what happens when you push down on a waterbed. People who diet know it as the yo-yo effect, economists as the downward spiral and biologists know it as the pork cycle.

To keep things closer to home, you can forbid a child to smoke, but doing so can effectively make smoking more attractive to the child. Your solution has become part of the problem.

All these phenomena can be compared to getting your car stuck in the mud. You try to drive it out, but the more you spin the wheels, the deeper down your car sinks.

*

Strike

A concert master was going through a series of difficult negotiations when he was confronted by union representatives who threatened to initiate a week-long strike, even though the orchestra was preparing for a very important concert which was scheduled for two days' time. The conflict was deadlocked until the concert master made them a paradoxical offer…

For the answer, look in the back of this booklet

Compensating feedback

Stuck-thinking is a simple concept in theory – turning a problem into a disaster – but in practice it can be difficult to recognize a stuck-thinking pattern, let alone break out of it. This has to do with what system theorists call 'compensating feedback'. It's like making a dent in a plastic bottle. For a moment something has changed, but soon enough the bottle will plop back into its original form.

We like to combat problems with direct and effective measures. If your child lacks confidence you believe you must speak to him encouragingly but unfortunately it's not that simple. Reality takes over and as we've already seen, a non-smoking rule just makes smoking more interesting, while nothing is more demoralising than parents giving 'motivational' monologues. Who, other than a loser, needs a motivational speech?

The difficulty lies in the fact that compensating feedback is almost always invisible as it happens

Those who say 'yes' are rewarded by the adventures they have, and those who say 'no' are rewarded by the safety they attain.

[Keith Johnstone]

At his wedding, a man was made a gift of a hideous painting by his mother-in-law. 'It will look lovely above the sofa', the mother-in-law said. Whereupon the son-in-law replied, 'In that case we'll have to move the sofa to the attic'.

outside our field of vision. Take for example a centre for difficult youths, where a particular group was causing lots of problems. The supervisors reacted by enacting harsher punishments which only resulted in the problematic group became even more troublesome. Then one of the supervisors started looking more closely at the situation and discovered that the youths considered the punishments to be badges of honour. Who dared to break the most rules? Who went furthest in challenging authority? In practice, the punishments were regarded as a reward, so the supervisors made the radical decision to stop punishing altogether. Within no time the bothersome behaviour had disappeared.

No matter how difficult it can be to recognize stuck-thinking, one thing is clear - more of the same will not work. Getting even angrier with your child, becoming stricter and stricter with your employees, trying harder and harder to lose weight, are all stuck-thinking patterns. As Einstein said, 'Insanity is doing the same things over and over again and expecting a different outcome.'

*

Delay

A second reason why it can be so difficult to recognize stuck-thinking has to do with the time-factor as it usually takes time for compensating feedback to be observed and understood. Sometimes, as with a plastic bottle, it's a matter of seconds but it can be a matter of months or even years.

Imagine you're overworked. Too much work to do and too little time in which to do it. You can solve that problem by working overtime. But if you don't tell your colleagues or your boss that your workload is too heavy, there's a good chance they will give you even more work to do. And if you try to solve that by working even harder, you'll find yourself in a vicious circle. In the short term your solution may appear to be working, but the tragedy is that in the long term your problem will only get bigger and bigger.

To take another example, imagine an organisation that's too bureaucratic, bound up in its own red tape. How would you solve that problem? Simple! You would divide the company into separate units, each with its own budget and powers so that the individual units become more decisive and effective. But the more the separate solutions work, the more a new problem makes itself felt, as the left hand doesn't know what the right hand is doing anymore. One unit may strictly enforce a certain policy but another unit may not be so precise and will come up with its own rules, and this in turn creates a new problem, the exact opposite of bureaucracy, anarchy. This 'new' problem is solved by creating more 'guidelines' and 'procedures' and so, many years later, the organisation is back to square one, bureaucracy.

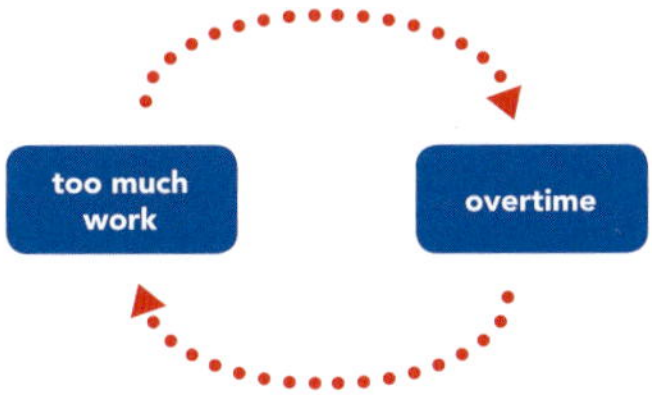

Initially, in the case of both examples, the action taken appears to be effectively solving the problem. However, to quote Peter Senge: 'Today's problems come from yesterday's solutions'.

*

Boot

Sometimes there are solutions to non-existing problems - a fascinating form of stuck-thinking as the 'solution' creates a problem.

In the United States all cars are required to have a 'trunk release' inside the boot (or trunk). The dynamic interplay of the little man, dotted line with arrow and the car, tells us we're dealing with a person fleeing the scene. But fleeing from what? Has he painfully stumbled and fallen into the boot and is now hastening to the pharmacy to buy some bandages? No, wait, it's an escape device. Should someone unexpectedly be kidnapped by a crime syndicate, he can always escape by opening the boot from the inside.

What a brilliant solution! And what an unfortunate setback for the criminals when they open the boot to find it empty! 'Mr. Smith is gone! What happened? Oh, we forgot about the escape device. Damn, that's the second time this month.'

*

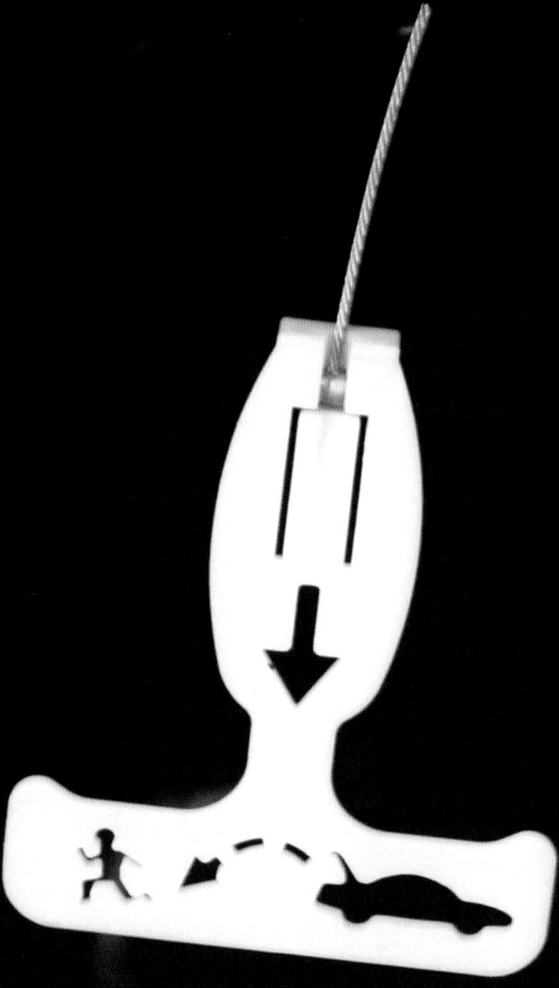

To the pessimist the glass is

half empty

'Flip-thinking' uses a third approach.

To the optimist the glass is

half full

where is the tap?

Omdenken

The big question is, if stuck-thinking doesn't work, what does? Of course pretending problems don't exist and sticking your head in the sand is not a solution. Luckily there's another, more creative way which has everything to do with how we face up to problems. How do we view a problem initially?

Are problems a challenge then? Certainly not! Some problems are simply a nuisance. For instance, some men go bald as they get older. Annoying! Say goodbye to that manly head of hair. Bad luck and misfortune exist whether we like it or not, it can't be helped and to resist, to say 'yes-but', doesn't help in those cases. Problems are an inescapable part of our lives but sometimes we can make the best of the situation, make a virtue of necessity and transform a problem into an opportunity. In our language, to 'flip-think' a problem. In Dutch, we call it 'omdenken'.

Flip-thinking is like an intellectual, philosophical form of jiu-jitsu. Problems can suddenly be used to your advantage. Strangely enough, you don't accomplish this by resisting the problem, but by saying 'yes' to it, by accepting it.

Saying 'yes' is the first step in flip-thinking, accepting the things you cannot change, turning a 'yes-but' into a 'yes'. By doing this, you turn a problem into a fact and with the second step you turn a 'yes' into a 'yes-and'. Transform the fact that's bothering you into a new opportunity. What does hair loss actually mean? It is what it is and once you have accepted the fact it depends on what you do with it. If you resist, the result will be a struggle, stress and irritation. If you say 'yes-and' to it, a new opportunity will appear. Perhaps being bald is the latest fashion.

From the moment you flip-think a situation, an interesting paradox appears. From then on, the bigger the problem the better and the more hair you lose, the better.

*

Yes-but

Yes-and

Flip-thinking

verb

flip•think•ing; flip thought;

: a (thinking) technique which is used to transform problems into opportunities; *synonym* yes-and-thinking; *antonym* yes-but-thinking, thinking in terms of threats and limitations

The board of directors managed to resolutely flip-think any doubts the press had; the psychiatrist advised the couple to flip-think the pattern of their relationship; after the trade union and the company flip thought their negotiations it appeared there had never been any disagreements.

Stuck-thinking

verb

stuck•think•ing; stuck thought;

: a way of thinking that enlarges problems, turning problems into disasters, getting stuck in one's own way of thinking; *antonym* flip-thinking, transforming problems into opportunities

The interim manager came to the conclusion that the organisation was constantly stuck-thinking itself; the lawyer said that his client stuck thought her relationships with men since an early age; the negotiator helped both parties by examining their process of stuck-thinking.

Problem

To flip-think a problem sounds simple but in practice it isn't. On the contrary we're constantly at a loss, as we tackle either the wrong problem or we tackle the problem wrongly. So let's take a small philosophical detour, to ask whether problems even exist at all. The word itself, 'problem', suggests that there is only one issue, which is a fallacy.

For example, one evening we're at home sitting comfortably on the sofa when suddenly the doorbell rings. It is annoying. At that moment we equate the doorbell with the problem. Doorbell equals problem. The reality is (unfortunately) more complex than that because a problem always consists of two things. The doorbell in itself is meaningless. The doorbell is just a fact. A given. The doorbell only becomes a problem when we couple it to the desire for a quiet evening. Because, let's be honest, if we were all alone and hoping for someone to finally pay us a visit, then the doorbell wouldn't be 'the problem', it would be 'the answer'.

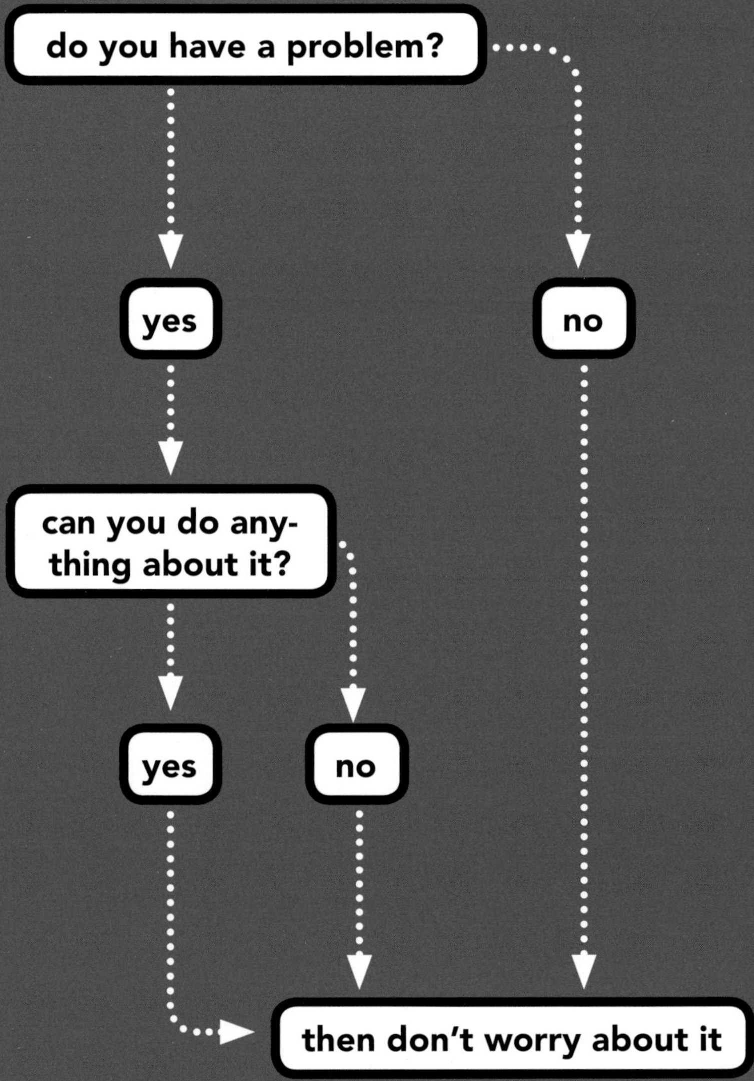
do you have a problem?
yes
no
can you do any-thing about it?
yes
no
then don't worry about it

Problems aren't the problem; our expectations are the problem.

Why is this insight so important? Because whenever we are confronted by a problem we tend to look beyond the immediate problem to the world around us. We feel that problems are things that 'happen' to us. As if we are unblemished and innocent and the world around us is constantly dumping all sorts of problems in our lap. When we take a closer look, however, it is our expectations that cause us to experience a fact as a problem.

The good news is that although we can't change facts, we can change our expectations. As soon as we can let go of the idea of what should be, we can often see, for the first time, what could be. Getting back to the doorbell - maybe it's a long lost love or a National Lottery camera crew waiting to tell you that you've won the jackpot, tax free, including a brand new BMW, all filled up and ready to go!

By the way, it could also be a bailiff, a debt collector come to seize that new car. That's the trouble. You don't know.

*

Camp

During a summer holiday camp an active camp leader is in charge of a rather passive group of children. No matter what activities she suggests, she fails to get the group to respond and the more enthusiastically she tries to motivate them, the more apathetically the group reacts. Then she discovers a different approach. Which one?

For the answer, look in the back of this booklet

Fact

A farmer and a scientist are sitting in a car. The farmer looks outside and says, 'Look, the sheep have been sheared'. 'Totally sheared?' the scientist asks. 'Yes,' the farmer answers, 'everybody can see that'. 'I'm not too sure of that,' the scientist says. 'The side we're looking at has been sheared, but whether we can say the same about the other side remains to be seen.'

Flip-thinking starts with knowing as much as possible about the facts, being able to see the difference between reality and our interpretation of reality, between that which 'is' and that which 'should be'. Mostly we see what we 'think' we see. Not even 5 percent of what we see is based on factual observation, the other 95 percent consists of memory, addition, omission and summarisation. To quote the Stoic philosopher Epictetus: 'Men are disturbed not by things, but by the view they take of them.'

To observe is difficult, but to observe the right things is even harder. The trick is not only seeing what you see, but also seeing what you don't see at first. To know what you need to know. For example, a group of youths tended to hang around a certain house. Nobody understood the attraction and when the police requested them to move to a nearby square, they were simply ignored. Then a youth councillor went searching for the 'unseen facts'.

What were the facts of the case? The youths clustered around the same house every day, because the residents had an open wireless network, no wi-fi password necessary. Once the councillor recognized this, he soon managed to flip-think the problem. The residents secured their wireless network with a password and at the nearby square the city council installed a (stronger and faster) free wireless access point, without a password, of course. What happened? Everybody was happy. The youths had their own place to hang out where they didn't bother anybody, and the police were saved many unnecessary calls.

*

A goat is attached to a two meter rope and six meters away lies a bale of hay. Still the goat manages to eat the hay. How is this possible?

Did I say the rope was attached to anything?

Perspective

Whether something is a problem or not, greatly depends on the perspective from which we choose to view the situation. One person's problem could be another person's opportunity. Three weeks of rain during a vacation is annoying but for a farmer that same rain could be a blessing, especially after a long drought. By the way, movie cinemas also love rainy summers, just like supermarkets love a recession. When people eat out less, they buy more food at the supermarket.

Before we label 'a problem' as 'a problem', we should consider whether our problem might not be someone else's opportunity and vice versa? For example, in the Dutch city of Haarlem a web-hosting company was spending a fortune each year on electricity to cool their computer servers. Meanwhile, a nearby cathedral was spending a fortune on heating costs. After learning about one another, they came up with a new concept, 'Holy Warming'. The church is warmed by the computer servers' excess heat, while servers are cooled by the chilly air in the church's cellar.

What is wrong here?
The horse is facing backwards.

River

A man is walking through the forest. At the edge of the forest he comes to a river. He looks for a bridge or some shallow water to cross over, but he can't find any. After a while he sees a farmer on the other side of the river and calls to him, 'Do you know how I can reach the other side?' The farmer answers, 'The other side? You're already there!'

The fact that your perspective decides how you experience an event, can lead to funny situations. For example, a father was bothered by the fact that whenever his eleven-year-old son had showered, the shower head was much too low. One morning he said to his son: 'Son, you know what's really bothering me? Every morning when I want to take a shower the shower head is too low. Could you put it back up after you shower?' The son listened attentively, was silent for a moment, and then answered, 'I'll do that, no problem. Now that you mention it though, I'd like to tell you something that's bothering me, if you don't mind. Every morning when I want to take a shower, the shower head is much too high. Could you please put it back down after you shower?'

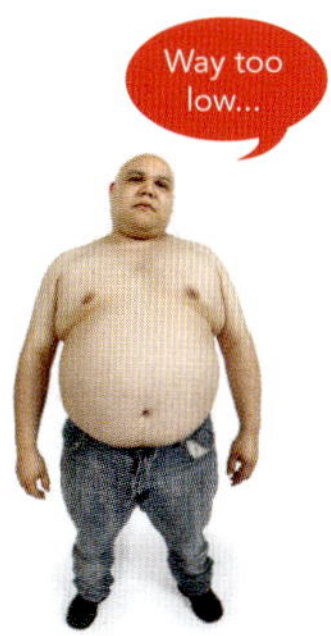

HEMA maps
Upside Down
World Map
www.hemamaps.com.au
Weddell Sea
Bellingshausen Sea
Antarctic Circle
Drake Passage
Scotia Sea
Cape Horn
Punta Arenas
ARGENTINA
CHILE
Santiago
Buenos Aires
Montevideo
URUGUAY
Rosario
Cordoba
Porto Alegre
Asuncion
PARAGUAY
Tropic of Capricorn
Sao Paulo
Rio de Janeiro
Sucre
BOLIVIA
La Paz
Brasilia
Salvador
BRAZIL
Lima
PERU
Recife
Fortaleza
Equator
Belém
Guayaquil
ECUADOR
Quito
Cali
Bogota
COLOMBIA
Medellin
French Guiana
Cayenne
Paramaribo
Georgetown
SURINAME
GUYANA
VENEZUELA
Caracas
Maracaibo
PANAMA
Panama
COSTA RICA
San Jose
Managua
NICARAGUA
EL SALVADOR
San Salvador
GUATEMALA
Guatemala
Tegucigalpa
HONDURAS
BELIZE
Belmopan
Kingston
JAMAICA
Port-au-Prince
HAITI
Santo Domingo
DOMINICAN REPUBLIC
San Juan
TRINIDAD & TOBAGO
Port of Spain
Caribbean Sea
CUBA
Havana
Acapulco
Mexico
Guadalajara
MEXICO
Monterrey
Tropic of Cancer
Sargasso Sea
Nassau
THE BAHAMAS
Miami
Gulf of Mexico
Houston
New Orleans
Baton Rouge
Austin
Tallahassee
Montgomery
Atlanta
Jackson
Dallas
El Paso
Phoenix
San Diego
Los Angeles
Columbia
Memphis
Little Rock
Oklahoma City
Santa Fe
Las Vegas
Raleigh
Washington
Nashville
Kansas City
Denver
San Francisco
Sacramento
Philadelphia
UNITED STATES OF AMERICA
Baltimore
New York
Cleveland
Indianapolis
Providence
Chicago
Lincoln
Salt Lake City
Boston
Albany
Detroit
Milwaukee
Concord
Toronto
Lansing
Cheyenne
Portland
Halifax
Montpelier
St Paul
Minneapolis
Pierre
Fredericton
Augusta
Ottawa
Charlottetown
Montreal
Bismarck
Seattle
Victoria
St John's
Quebec
Lake Superior
Winnipeg
Regina
Vancouver
Calgary
Happy Valley-Goose Bay
Lake Winnipeg
Saskatoon
Edmonton
Schefferville
Labrador Sea
Hudson Bay
Churchill
CANADA
Juneau
Gulf of Alaska
Whitehorse
Anchorage
Bethel
Nuuk
Hudson Strait
Great Slave Lake
Iqaluit
Yellowknife
Alaska (U. S. A.)
Davis Strait
Echo Bay
Great Bear Lake
Dawson
Fairbanks
Nome
Foxe Basin
Bathurst Inlet
Arctic Circle
Repulse Bay
Baffin Island
Inuvik
Cambridge Bay
Victoria Island
Beaufort Sea
Sachs Harbour
Banks Island
Baffin Bay
Devon Island
Melville Island
Greenland (Denmark)
Parry Islands
Queen Elizabeth Islands
Ellesmere Island
ARCTIC OCEAN
SOUTH PACIFIC OCEAN
NORTH PACIFIC OCEAN
Easter Is
French Polynesia
Galapagos Is
Hawaiian Islands
Honolulu
Dunedin
Invercargill
Christchurch
South Island
Wellington
Napier
Rotorua
Hamilton
Auckland
North Island
NEW ZEALAND
Chatham Is
New Caledonia
Noumea
Nuku'alofa
TONGA
Suva
FIJI
Port-Vila
VANUATU
Apia
SAMOA
Vaiaku
TUVALU
SOLOMON ISLANDS
KIRIBATI
NAURU
Yaren
Bairiki
Delap-Uliga-Djarrit
MARSHALL ISLANDS
INTERNATIONAL DATE LINE
Aleutian Islands
Bering Sea
Petropavlovsk-Kamchatskiy
Providenya
Ust' Penzhino
Bering Strait
Chukchi Sea
Pevek
East Siberian Sea
40°
60°
80°
100°
120°
140°
160°
180°
20°
0°

ANTARCTICA
SOUTHERN OCEAN
INDIAN OCEAN
SOUTH ATLANTIC OCEAN
NORTH ATLANTIC OCEAN
LEGEND
• Capital • City, Town
Traditional World Maps are drawn from the perspective of the first European explorers and cartographers – with the Northern Hemisphere at the top.
We think its time to break with tradition and show the world from the perspective of all those people living in the Southern Hemisphere.
After all, there is no ancient geographical feature saying "This way up".
© Hema Maps Pty Ltd 2009 10th Edition
Hema Maps Pty Ltd
PO Box 4365 Eight Mile Plains,
Brisbane, QLD 4113 Australia
Ph: +61 7 3340 0000 Fax: +61 7 3340 0099
www.hemamaps.com
manager@hemamaps.com.au
Hema Maps NZ Limited
PO Box 58924 Greenmount, East Tamaki,
Auckland, New Zealand
Ph: +64 9 273 6459 Fax: +64 9 273 6479
sales@hemamaps.co.nz
Hema Maps North America
921 E. 86th Street, Suite 107, Indianapolis IN 46240, USA
ph: +1 (317) 257-HEMA (4362) Fax: +1 (317) 257-5362
info@hemamaps.com
Abbreviations:
B.-HERZ. - BOSNIA AND HERZEGOVINA
KO. - KOSOVO
LIE. - LIECHTENSTEIN
LUX. - LUXEMBOURG
MAC. - MACEDONIA
MONT. - MONTENEGRO
RUS. FED. - RUSSIAN FEDERATION
RUSSIAN FEDERATION
CHINA
MONGOLIA
KAZAKHSTAN
INDIA
INDONESIA
MALAYSIA
PHILIPPINES
IRAN
SAUDI ARABIA
TURKEY
UKRAINE
SUDAN
CHAD
NIGER
MALI
ALGERIA
LIBYA
EGYPT
ETHIOPIA
KENYA
TANZANIA
ANGOLA
ZAMBIA
NAMIBIA
BOTSWANA
REPUBLIC OF SOUTH AFRICA
MADAGASCAR
SWEDEN
NORWAY
FINLAND
ICELAND
SPAIN
FRANCE
ITALY
GERMANY
POLAND
UNITED KINGDOM
IRELAND
Greenland
Svalbard (Norway)
Barents Sea
Kara Sea
Laptev Sea
Norwegian Sea
Mediterranean Sea
Arabian Sea
Bay of Bengal
South China Sea
Timor Sea
Gulf of Guinea
Bay of Biscay
Franz Josef Land

Reverse

In the book *Huh?! The Dutch Art of Flip-thinking*, I write about fifteen different strategies for flip-thinking a problem, too many to list in this booklet but that doesn't mean I can't cherry pick the best ones for you. What are the most effective strategies? Here are the top three, the best of flip-thinking.

The most effective strategy is that of reversal. Is ADHD a handicap or maybe a talent? Not a strange question if you think about it. Some comedians wouldn't be nearly as funny if they didn't benefit from a little ADHD.

I'll give you another example involving ADHD. A father is asked to help at one of his five-year-old daughter's class activities. The teacher has organised a walk in the forest but before they go into the forest, the teacher takes the father to one side and points to one of the children. 'That's Johnny. Johnny has ADHD so watch him carefully or he'll wander off into the woods. Last weekend his parents lost him for two whole hours. Please keep an eye on him, because he can't be trusted.' The

Children with ADHD have a serious problem. All their teachers are boring.

father however decides to look at the situation differently. He sits the young lad in the back of his car and looks him in the eye. 'Johnny, I have a problem. We're going into the forest. Now you might think that I look like a strong and fearless dad, but I have to tell you that I'm scared to death of the forest. Would you please keep an eye on me?' As soon as they enter the forest, little Johnny grabs the father's hand. The whole walk Johnny stays at his side, beaming with pride because he is entrusted with taking care of the big fearless dad.

*

I destroy my enemies
when I make them my friends.

Goliath

When the Israelites set eyes on Goliath for the first time they said, 'He is so large, we will never defeat him'. But David said,

'He is so large,
I will never miss.'

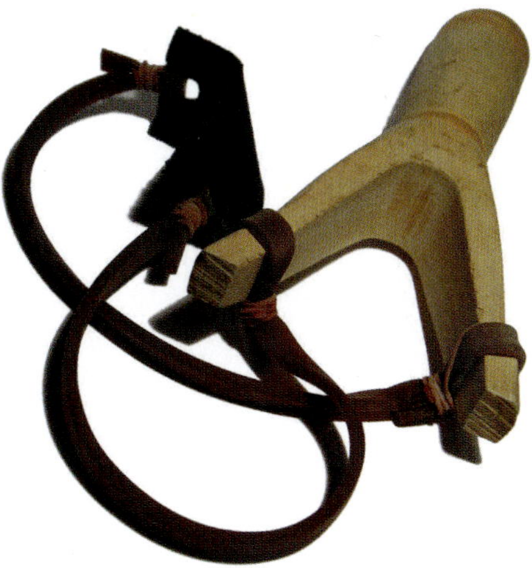

Witch

A psychiatrist in Baltimore had a patient that was convinced she was a witch. She said she was the reincarnation of Anna Göldi, the last woman in Europe to be convicted of witchcraft, sentenced to death and burned at the stake in Switzerland in 1782. No matter how desperately her friends and family tried to tell her otherwise, she stuck to her story. She was the one and only Anna Göldi. Still, the psychiatrist managed to change her mind. How did he do it?

For the answer, look in the back of this booklet

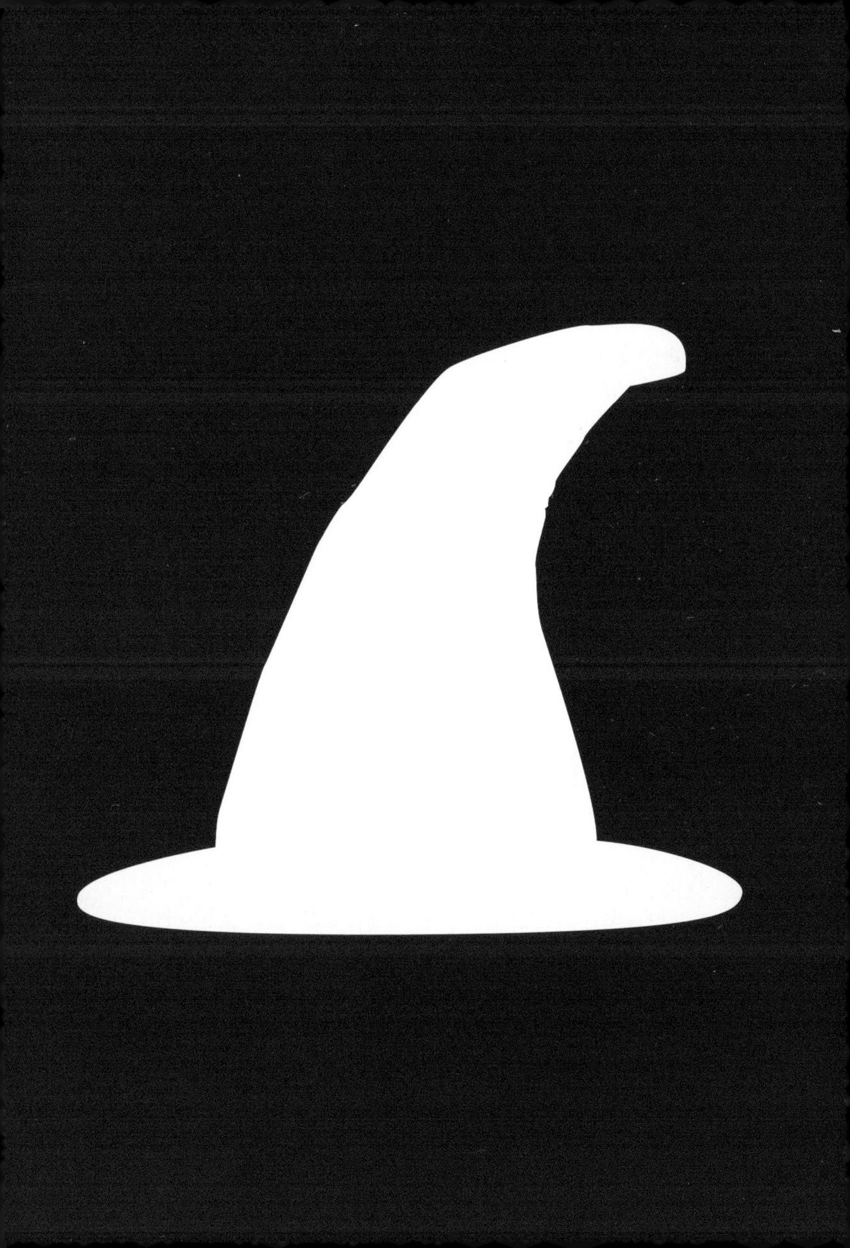

Ally

The second flip-thinking strategy is that of collaboration. You can fight your enemies, but you can also turn them into allies. Like when the police catch criminals by using criminal informants.

The United Stated Department of Defense has decided that cybersecurity is a top priority. What do they do to achieve a highly secured computer network? Declare war on all hackers? Quite the opposite, they recruit them. Each year the Department of Defense organises a hacking competition, where the best hackers can expect rewards of up to a million dollars. This way the U.S. government is always aware of the newest and best hacking techniques and they know who to keep an eye on or, even better, recruit.

We can also transform our own body from an enemy into an ally. There was a woman who, for over two years, had fought unbearable pain in her back. She had seen everyone, from a GP to a physiotherapist to a rheumatologist. Not even intensive rehabilitation therapy helped. A clear cause of the pain (or a solution to it) was never found. Dispirited and frustrated about her dysfunctional body, she decided to turn things around. Instead of fighting pain as her enemy, she made it her ally. She told us this:

'Every morning I wake up feeling pain, which reminds me to take extra special care of myself. I take my time getting up. Focus on breathing in and out. Do several stretching exercises to awaken my whole body. I eat nutritiously. I'm thankful for the fact that I can use my legs. I try to make sure I stay balanced throughout the day. For example, I'll lie down for ten minutes whenever I feel tiredness setting in, or I'll go for a short walk when I feel I need it. This way the pain has been transformed into an ally that ensures I take good care of myself, stay focused on what I really need, know my limitations and above all it lets me cherish the nicer moments in my life.'

Keep your friends close, but your enemies closer.

from The Godfather, 1972

Wu-wei

In the West, we tend to think we can change things by doing, by taking action, by rolling up our sleeves.

When it comes to flip-thinking, however, inaction is just as important as action. Sometimes you can change things by doing nothing. Or – on the other hand – things may not change, no matter how much you do. Doing nothing can be an effective strategy, waiting, biding your time, being patient.

In Taoism this attitude of action through inaction is known as 'wu wei', which literally means 'not acting against nature'. Its roots can be traced to observations of the workings of nature, grass just grows and a bird just flies without any discernable effort. In nature everything moves in harmony with a particular energy and in a certain direction. Taoism states that our actions often disrupt this natural harmony. You could call that stuck-thinking.

Inaction isn't just doing nothing, it's a conscious choice to not act for the time being, to wait, a form of inaction which requires a certain alertness. The results can be surprising. The grass is at its highest when we return from vacation.

*

To disrupt

The most enjoyable strategy is that of disruption. At an early age we are programmed to expect certain things from the world. We are told how things should be. Finish your dinner. Be home before dark. Listen to your teacher. These are the rules. But who says you should follow the rules?

If we want to flip-think, we need to examine every assumption we have made in our lives. How do we think? What are our convictions? Where are our blind spots? Sometimes one plus one equals three or fifteen or kiwi. Being aware of the rules of the game is not as important as knowing when you can bend, break, or manipulate those rules.

A while ago, train drivers in Sweden were forbidden to wear shorts to work as their employer had decided they dressed too informally. Luckily, men and women in Sweden have equal rights, so the next day, the male train drivers turned up for work wearing… skirts.

*

As soon as I
knew my limits,
I pushed myself
beyond them.

Zeneca

The employees of a chemical plant in Zeneca, Italy, are required to wear safety glasses. Despite this rule, hardly anybody wears them and after working in the same environment for many years, they tend to underestimate the possible dangers of their workplace. The workers also think the glasses are ugly and uncomfortable. Mandatory training courses, official warnings or fines don't seem to have any effect. What to do?

For the answer, look in the back of this booklet

As soon as I
knew my limits,
I pushed myself
beyond them.

Zeneca

The employees of a chemical plant in Zeneca, Italy, are required to wear safety glasses. Despite this rule, hardly anybody wears them and after working in the same environment for many years, they tend to underestimate the possible dangers of their workplace. The workers also think the glasses are ugly and uncomfortable. Mandatory training courses, official warnings or fines don't seem to have any effect. What to do?

For the answer, look in the back of this booklet

Problem? Idea!

Finally, flip-thinking is more of an art than a science. It takes patience and practice to get really good at it, just like learning how to play chess, ski, or play an instrument. However starting today, there is one effective reversal that you can apply right away, by turning a problem into 'the whole idea'.

You have a 'lazy son'? Maybe he's supposed to be like that and needs time to think, to work out ideas and decide about his future. You have a partner that doesn't talk much? Again, maybe that's how it's supposed to be. Perhaps you need to be quiet more often. You have problems at work? What if that's the sign that you need to find a new job? You have problems with your rebellious daughter? Maybe you need to finally let go of her.

The paradox is usually that the more you resist the way things are, the more you maintain the status quo. On the other hand, sincere and profound acceptance of reality usually leads to change.

*

BERT: 'Ernie, we have a problem. The car is broken.'
ERNIE: 'What do you mean a problem? We can play garage!'

It's not about colouring inside the lines it's about creating your own drawing.

Answers

Strike The concert master gave the orchestra a week off work. As he expected, they didn't like this as they didn't want to miss the important concert. The union representative then called for all the musicians to go on strike immediately, because they had 'the right to work'. This move resulted in her losing the support of the musicians and the conflict was resolved – without her mediation – in one short meeting.

Camp One day the camp leader stopped thinking of new activities. Within an hour the children were so bored that they were begging the camp leader to give them something to do.

Witch The psychiatrist built a stake and pyre.

Zeneca A well-known designer of sunglasses was asked to design a new line of safety glasses. The new glasses were so popular that people not only wore them at work, but also in their free time.

If we don't
get lost
we'll never find
a new route.

[Joan Littlewood]

What do children do
when it rains?

What do adults do when it rains?

Do you want to learn how to omdenk?

Reading about Omdenken is one thing, but experiencing it live will blow you away.

See one of our intelligent seminars, experience an awesome, mind-altering omdenk-training or participate in one of our hilarious, life-changing and unforgettable workshops.

Visit Omdenken.com for more information.